# BEGINNING
## UKULELE KIDS SONGBOOK
### With 10 Classic children songs

TERRY CARTER
**UKELIKETHEPROS**

**Guitars** and Ukes **in the Classroom**™
*Better Learning through Music*

UKELIKETHEPROS

# CONTENTS

ISBN-13: **978-1-7359692-8-2**
© 2022 Terry Carter
**By TERRY CARTER**
**UKELIKETHEPROS.COM**

DESIGNED BY: **@mapcontents**

# HOW TO READ TAB

Tablature (TAB) is a form of music reading for ukulele that uses a 4 line staff and numbers. Each line of the staff represents a string on the ukulele and the numbers represent which fret you play on. When looking at the TAB staff it reads like it's upside down on the paper compared to the strings of your ukulele. On the TAB staff, the highest line (closest to the sky) represents the 1st string (G string in **OPEN C TUNING**) of the ukulele, while the lowest line (closest to the ground) represents the 4th string (G string) of the ukulele. When you see 2 or more notes stacked on top of each other on the TAB staff, that means you play those notes at the same time, like a a chord.

## UKULELE STRINGS

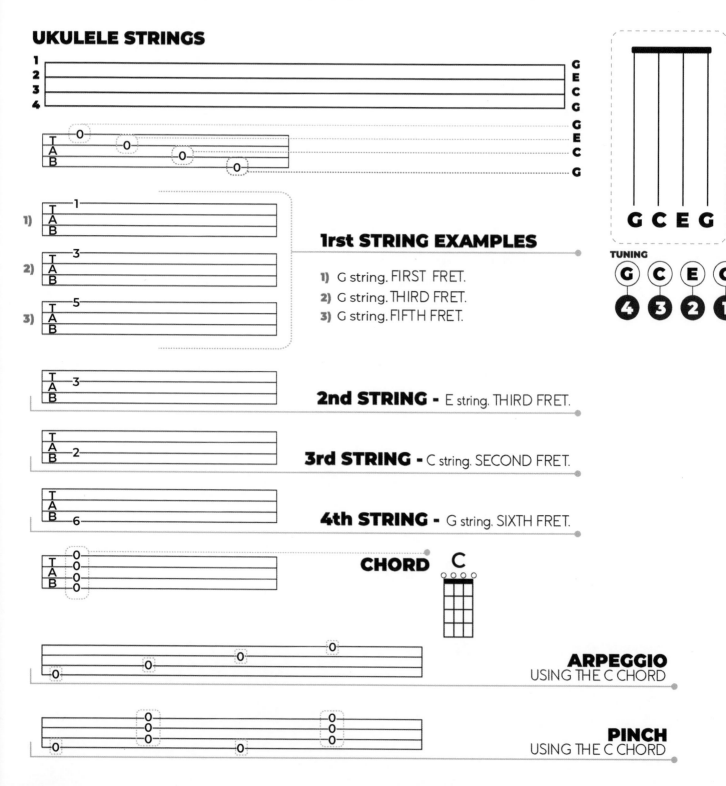

### 1rst STRING EXAMPLES

1) G string. FIRST FRET.
2) G string. THIRD FRET.
3) G string. FIFTH FRET.

**2nd STRING -** E string. THIRD FRET.

**3rd STRING -** C string. SECOND FRET.

**4th STRING -** G string. SIXTH FRET.

**CHORD**

**ARPEGGIO**
USING THE C CHORD

**PINCH**
USING THE C CHORD

# UNDERSTANDING THE SONG SHEETS

It is important to learn and memorize these terms and symbols because they not only apply to ukulele but to all music.

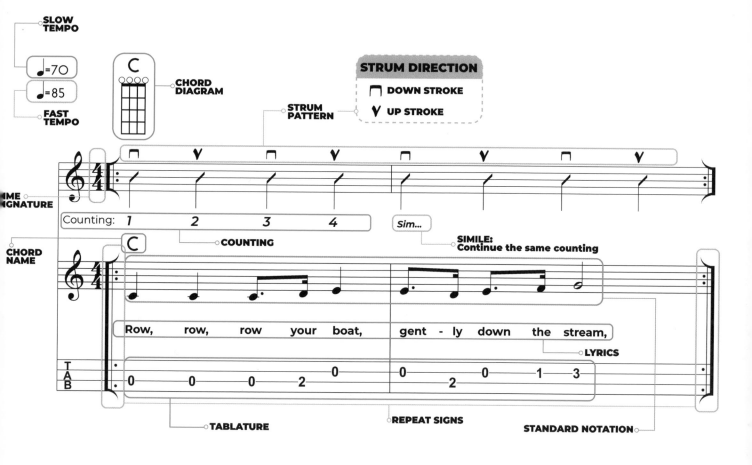

# UNDERSTANDING RHYTHMS

The main rhythms in this book are quarter notes, eighth notes, and sixteenth notes.

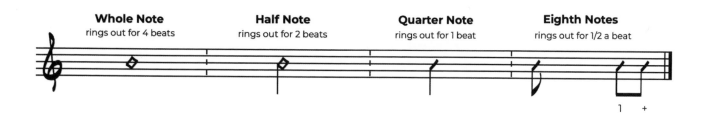

# UKULELE PARTS

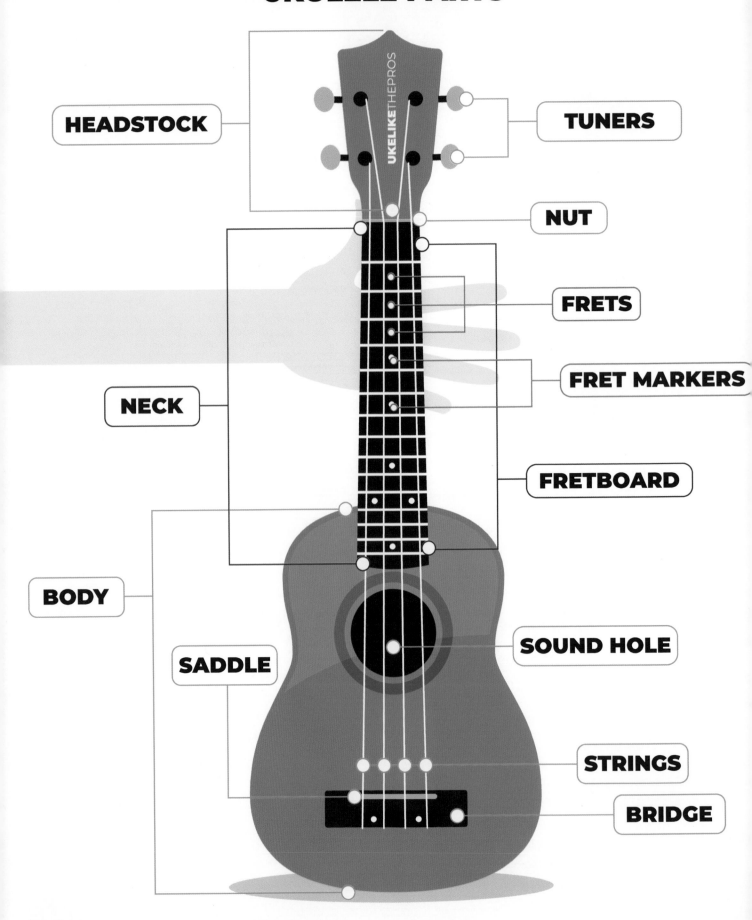

HEADSTOCK

TUNERS

NUT

FRETS

FRET MARKERS

NECK

FRETBOARD

BODY

SADDLE

SOUND HOLE

STRINGS

BRIDGE

# UKULELE HANDS

When playing fingerstyle on your ukulele, you will see both letters and numbers to indicate which fingers to use both for picking hand and your fretting hand. These letters and numbers will show up in the music notation, TAB, and/or chord diagrams.

| FRETTING HAND | PICKING HAND |
|---|---|
| The left hand for right-handed players will be indicated in the music or chord diagrams by numbers:<br>**1**=Index finger **3**=Ring finger<br>**2**=Middle finger **4**=Pinky finger | The right hand for right-handed players will be indicated in the music by letters:<br>**p**=Thumb **m**=middle<br>**i**=index **a**=ring **c**=pinky (not used in this course) |

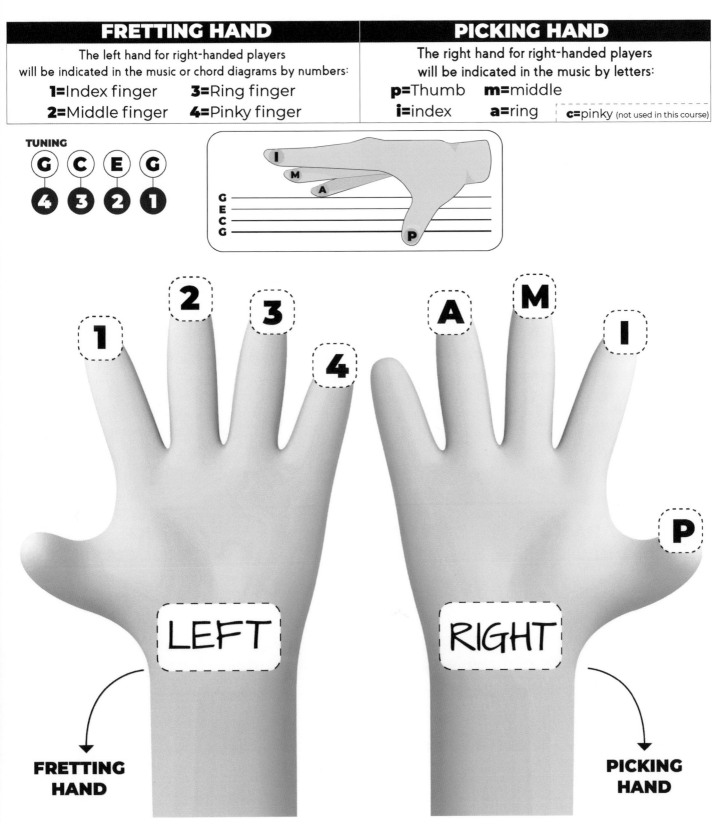

# UKULELE SIZES

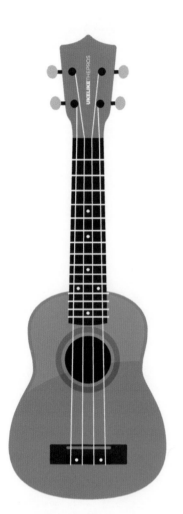

**SOPRANO**
LENGTH **21"**

**CONCERT**
LENGTH **24"**

**TENOR**
LENGTH **26"**

You can find a huge collection of ukuleles with different sizes, colors and woods in the **#1 Music Store:**

**TERRYCARTERMUSICSTORE.COM**

# HOW TO HOLD YOUR UKULELE

One of the first things you need to know before starting to play the ukulele is how to hold it. Start by placing the body of the ukulele on your leg, then, follow these recommendations:

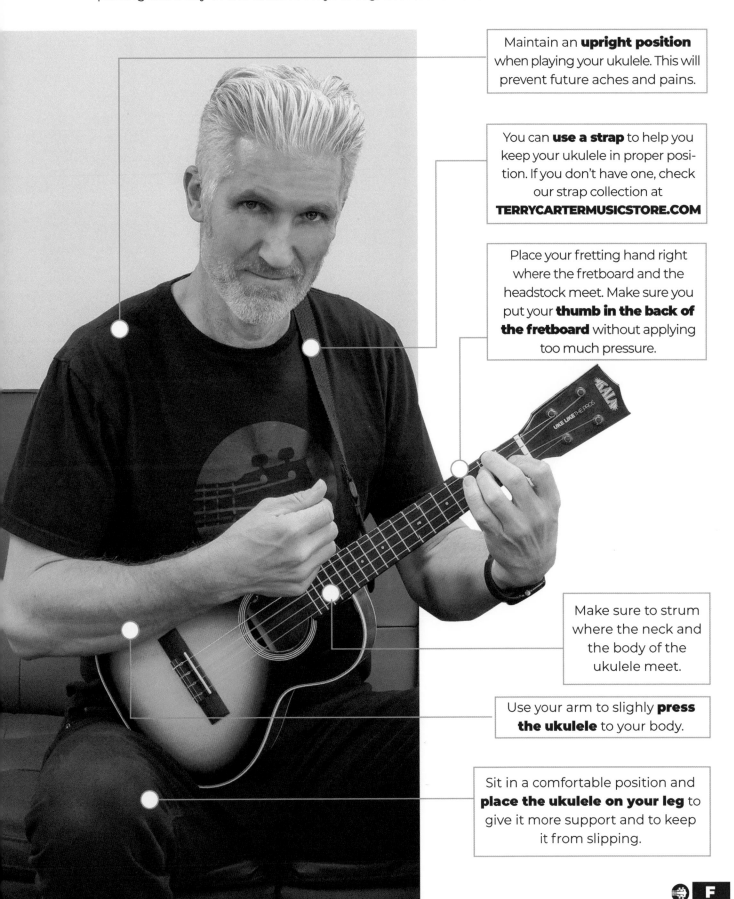

Maintain an **upright position** when playing your ukulele. This will prevent future aches and pains.

You can **use a strap** to help you keep your ukulele in proper position. If you don't have one, check our strap collection at **TERRYCARTERMUSICSTORE.COM**

Place your fretting hand right where the fretboard and the headstock meet. Make sure you put your **thumb in the back of the fretboard** without applying too much pressure.

Make sure to strum where the neck and the body of the ukulele meet.

Use your arm to slighly **press the ukulele** to your body.

Sit in a comfortable position and **place the ukulele on your leg** to give it more support and to keep it from slipping.

# HOW TO STRUM YOUR UKULELE

Use the thumb or the index finger of your strumming hand to lightly strum the strings. Learn the symbols and the difference between the up stroke and down stroke. Practice both up and down movements to get a better and smoother sound on your ukulele.

## WITH YOUR THUMB

Use the thumb of your strumming hand to play the strings together in a gentle move that will go **DOWN** from the 4th string to the 1st string of your ukulele. Use your flesh and part of your fingernail to get a nice and full sound out of the strings.

This movement is called **DOWN STROKE** and it's presented in music notation with this symbol:

DOWN

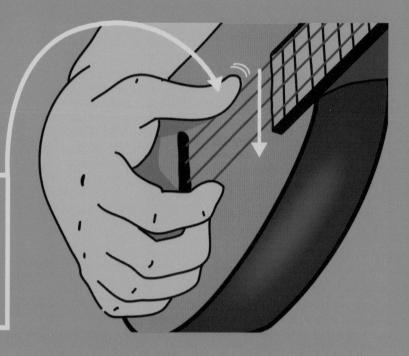

## WITH YOUR INDEX

Use the index finger of your strumming hand to play the strings together in a gentle move that will go **UP AND DOWN** from the 4th string to the 1st string, and from the 1st string back to the 4th string of your ukulele. Use your flesh and part of your fingernail to get a nice and full sound out of the strings.

These movements are called UP STROKE AND DOWN STROKE and are presented in music notation with these symbols:

DOWN     UP

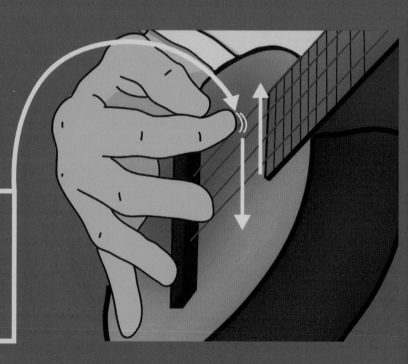

# NOTES ON THE UKULELE NECK
## OPEN C TUNING

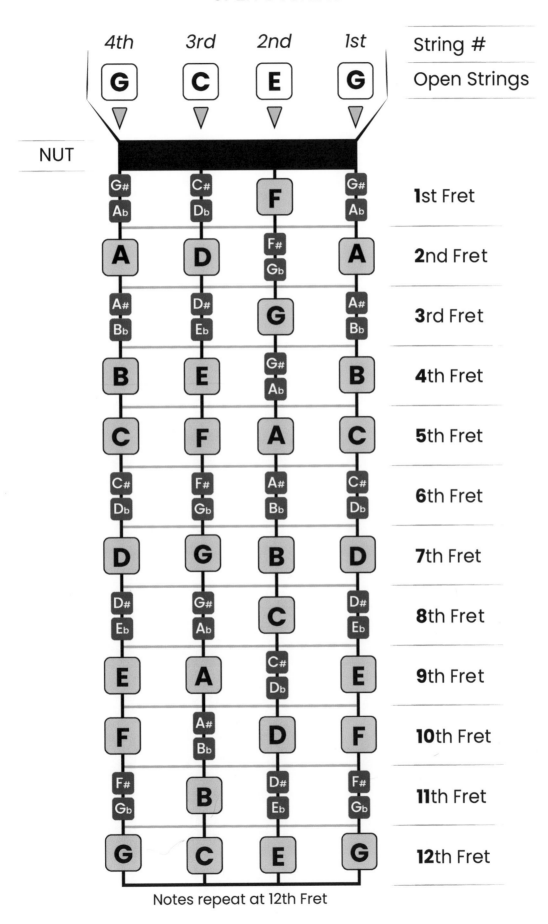

Notes repeat at 12th Fret

# CHORD CHART OPEN C TUNING

These are the most common chords you'll see in a great number of kid's songs. We've adapted the chords to the open C tuning method so it's easier for you to learn the shapes and have fun with your favorite songs.

# UNDERSTANDING CHORD DIAGRAMS
## OPEN C TUNING

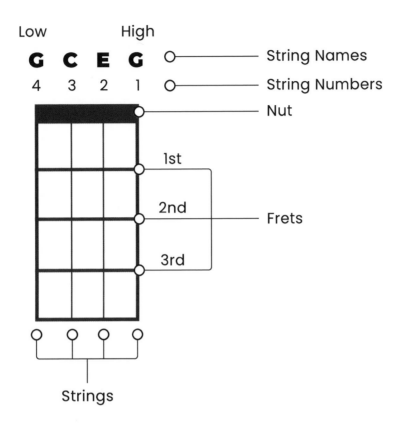

Low          High

G  C  E  G  ○———— String Names

4  3  2  1  ○———— String Numbers

○———— Nut

1st

2nd  ———— Frets

3rd

Strings

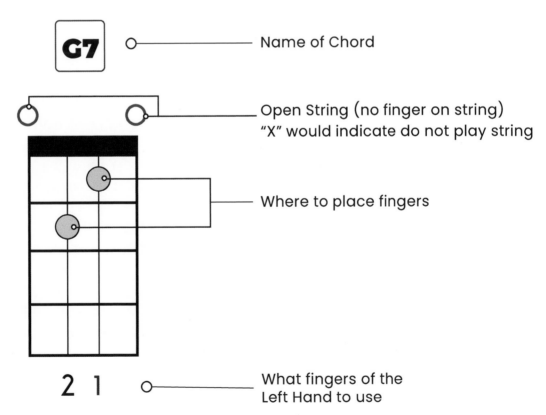

**G7**  ○———— Name of Chord

○          ○———— Open String (no finger on string)
"X" would indicate do not play string

———— Where to place fingers

2  1  ○———— What fingers of the
Left Hand to use

# BEGINNING
## UKULELE KIDS SONGBOOK
### With 10 Classic children songs

Finally, a complete Beginning Ukulele Kids Course Songbook that will teach kids and beginning ukulele players how to play ukulele in a fun and easy way. By the end of this songbook you will learn how to play 10 of the most popular children songs using the most used chords and strum patterns on the ukulele.

With special thanks to Guitars In The Classroom, the Beginning Ukulele Kids Course Songbook teaches how to play the ukulele in the open C tuning. The open C tuning makes learning and playing the ukulele easy and perfect for kids and the beginner. The open C tuning tunes the strings of the ukulele to G-C-E-G so that you get a C major chord simple by strumming all the open strings. The Open C tuning means even the youngest kid can easily strum the C chord and start playing songs as they develop their technique and coordination.

Thanks to the work of Guitars In The Classroom founder Jessica Baron, and Korg Education, the open C tuning has been proven to work on thousands of younger students to make ukulele fun and assessible. The open C tuning also makes playing chords—not only the C, but the other popular chords such as the F and G7—simple, because you only have to add one or two fingers to the fretboard. By knowing these 3 simple chords, the C, F, and G7, you can play hundreds of children's songs.

The Beginning Ukulele Kids Course Songbook teaching method is not only great for kids of all ages, but also works great for parents who want to play along and learn with their children, for the classroom teacher, for the beginner that is starting later in life, for anyone with hand, wrist, shoulder or arm problems, and for those who love nursery rhyme songs.

The Beginning Ukulele Kids Course Songbook will teach you 10 of the classic children songs in a step-by-step, easy to understand teaching method. Each lesson will build upon the next as you gain confidence in your strumming, counting, switching chords, rhythm, and technique, all while playing fun, popular songs. This songbook will show you how to strum each song with the correct rhythm, show you easy to read chord diagrams, and show you the lyrics and the melody in both standard notation and TAB.

The 10 all-time classic children's songs you will learn are:
- Frere Jacques/Are You Sleeping?
- Merrily We Roll Along/Mary Had A Little Lamb
- Row, Row, Row Your Boat
- This Old Man

The Wheels On The Bus
Old MacDonald
London Bridge
Itsy Bitsy Spider
Do Your Ears Hang Low
Twinkle Twinkle Little Star

Each song in this book will focus on learning new chords and strum patterns. By the end of this book you will not only know 10 of the all-time classic children's songs, but also be able to play the most widely used chords and strum patterns on the ukulele. This will be a great launching pad for you and your child as you journey into the magical world of ukulele. As part of this book, the play-along backing tracks are available to you at **ukelikethepros.com/kids-book**.
A complete step-by-step video course (sold separately) is also available at **ukelikethepros.com/kids**

The Beginning Ukulele Kids Course Songbook is the most structured book for learning the ukulele for kids. Each lesson and song is hand selected by ukulele master, Terry Carter. Terry is the founder of ukelikethepros.com and store.ukelikethepros.com, and has taken the techniques that helped him become the #1 online ukulele instruc-tor and put them into one comprehensive beginning book for kids.

Terry spent over 20 years as a Los Angeles studio musician, producer, and writer, working with greats such as Weezer, Josh Groban, Robby Krieger (The Doors), 2-time Grammy winning composer Christopher Tin (Calling All Dawns), Duff McKagan (Guns N' Roses), Grammy winning producer Charles Goodan (Santana/Rolling Stones), and the Los Angeles Philharmonic.
Terry has written and produced tracks for commercials (Discount Tire and Puma) and TV shows, including Scorpion (CBS), Pit Bulls & Parolees (Animal Planet), Trippin', Wildboyz, and The Real World (MTV). He has self-published more than 15 books for Uke Like The Pros and Rock Like The Pros, filmed over 30 ukulele and guitar online courses, and has millions of views on his social media channels. Terry received a Master of Music in Studio/Jazz Guitar Performance from University of Southern California, and a Bachelor of Music from San Diego State University, with an emphasis in Jazz Studies and Music Education. He has taught at the University of Southern California, San Diego State University, Santa Monica College, Miracosta College, and Los Angeles Trade Tech College.

**Practice Tip:**
Practice all these exercises slowly to make sure you play them correctly, accurately, and with the proper fingers. Also... Have fun!

# 01 - HOPSCOTCH

**By Terry Carter**

This song will help you switch between the C and the F chords. To play the C chord, strum all the open strings, and to play the F chord just place your 1st finger (index finger) on the 1st fret of the 2nd string. Strum both chords with your thumb using a downstroke (towards the ground). The strum pattern uses a whole note, strum on beat 1 and let the chord ring out for beats 1-2-3-4.

# 02 - THREE THUMBS UP

**By Terry Carter**

This song will add the G7 chord to the C and F chords you already know. It is easy to get from the F chord to the G7 chord. All you have to do is play the F chord and then add your 2nd finger (middle finger) to the 2nd fret of the 3rd string. Work on getting all three of these chords memorized as you will see them over and over again.

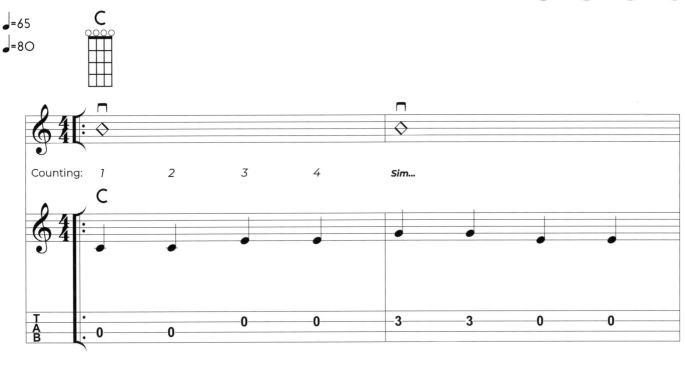

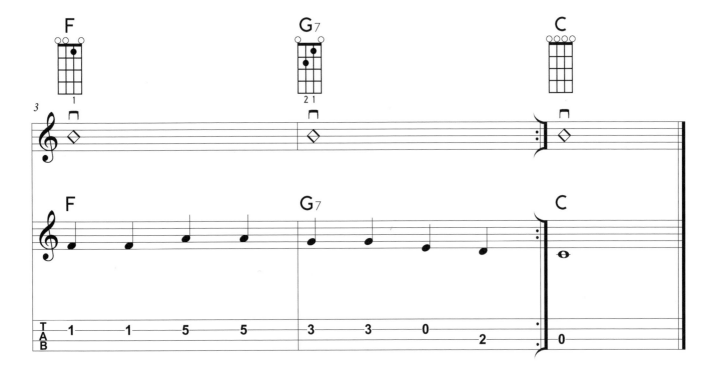

**By Terry Carter**

This song will work on switching between the C and the G7 chords. The C chord is easy but it will take some time to play the G7 chord because you have to place two fingers down on the fingerboard at the same time. Practice slowly and develop the finger memory to play the G7 chord.

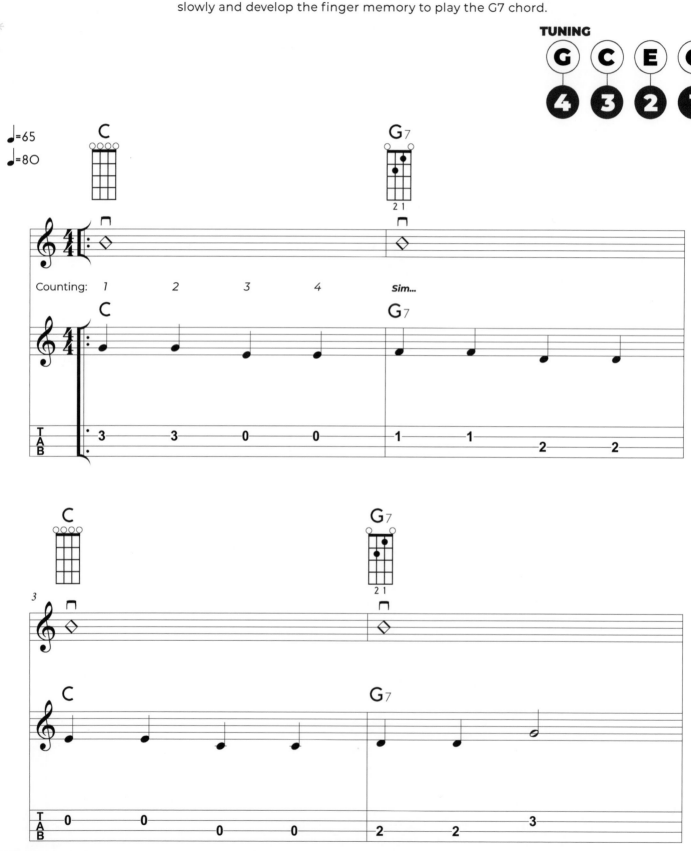

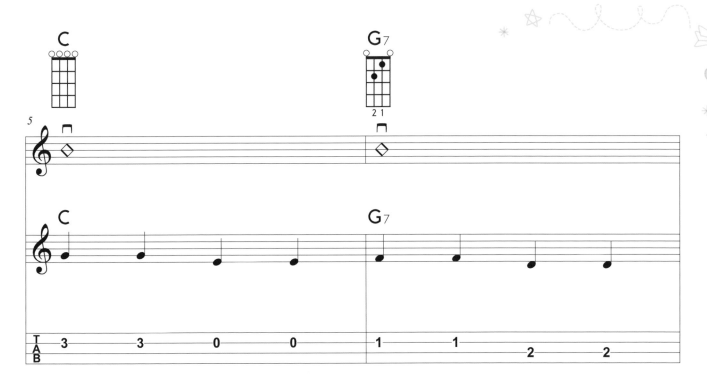

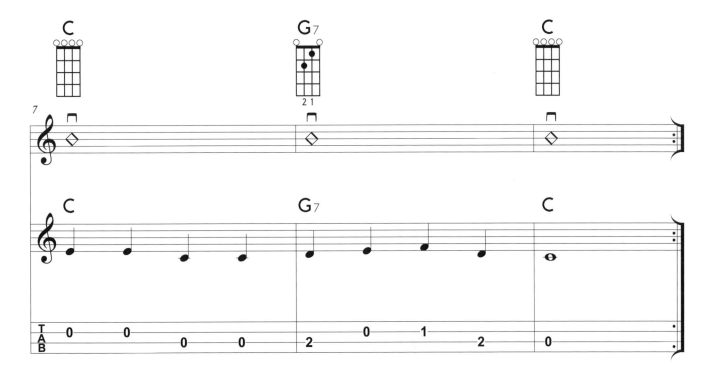

You can post your progress and see how others are doing at the **UKELIKETHEPROS.COM** Forum.

You can also get free access to the backing tracks at:
**UKELIKETHEPROS.COM/KIDS-BOOK**

# 04 - FRERE JACQUES / ARE YOU SLEEPING?

**Traditional**

This song will only use one chord, the C chord, for the entire song. Use a downstroke with your thumb to strum each chord using quarter notes. Quarter notes get one beat which means you will strum on every beat of the song. We use both the French and the English words.

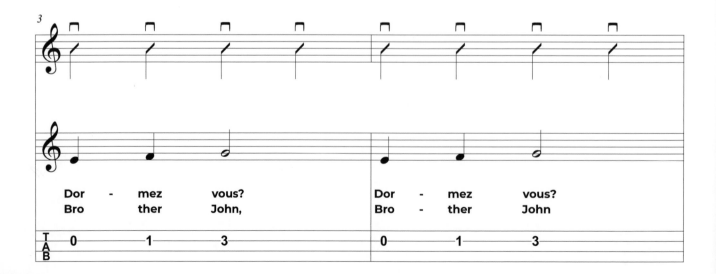

C

Son - nez  les  ma - ti - nes,
Morn - ing  bells  are  ring - ing,

Son - nez  les  ma - ti - nes
Morn - ing  bells  are  ring - ing,

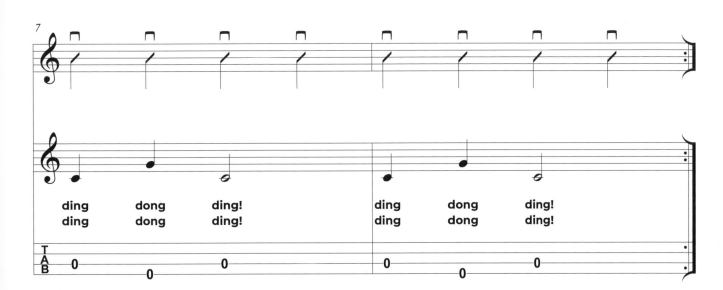

ding    dong    ding!
ding    dong    ding!

ding    dong    ding!
ding    dong    ding!

**Traditional**

This song will add the G7 chord. The rhythm has a quarter note on beats 1 and 2, and a half note on beat 3, which gives you some extra time to get to the G7 chord. You can use both Merrily We Roll Along and Mary Had A Little Lamb for this song.

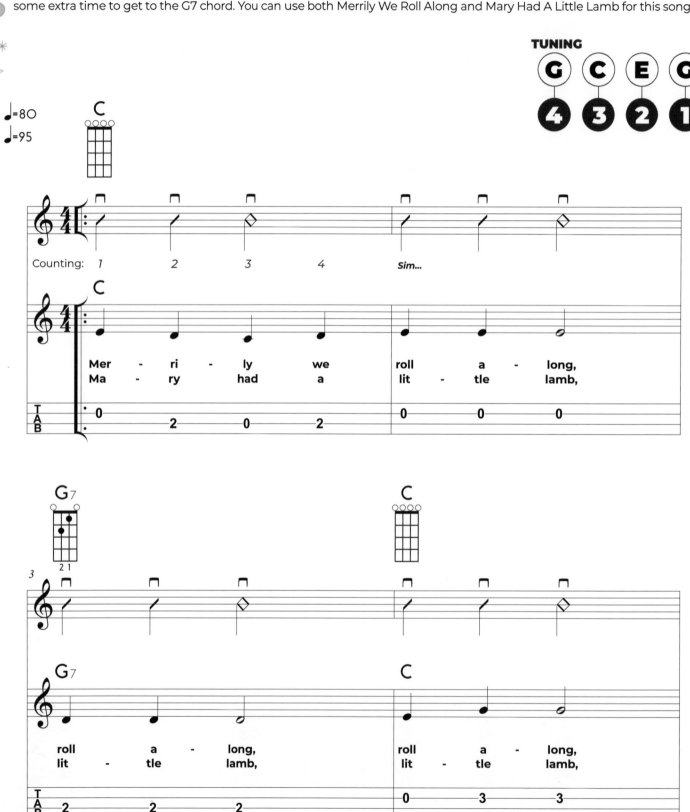

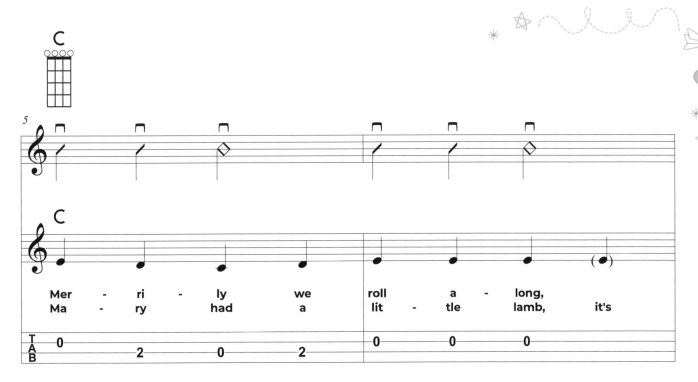

Mer - ri - ly we roll a - long,
Ma - ry had a lit - tle lamb, it's

o'er the deep blue sea.
fleece is white as snow.

You can post your progress and see how others are doing at the **UKELIKETHEPROS.COM** Forum.

You can also get free access to the backing tracks at: **UKELIKETHEPROS.COM/KIDS-BOOK**

# 06 - ROW, ROW, ROW YOUR BOAT

**Traditional**

This is a short song, only 4 measures long. It only uses the C and G7 chords but will use all quarter notes for the rhythm.
Once you memorize the G7 chord, it will make it easier to switch between the C and G7 chords.

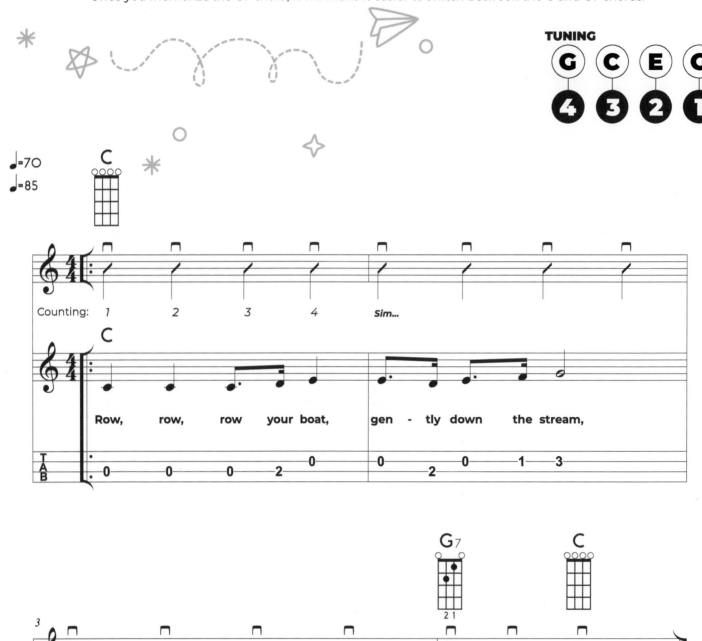

# TIME TO HAVE SOME
# FUN!

## FIND AND CIRCLE ALL THE 8 UKULELES

It is time to exercise our brain with a cool game called "FIND THE UKE!". All you have to do is stare carefully at the image below and help me find the 8 ukuleles I lost in the kid's room! Let's work together so we can find them all!

**Find all the answers on PAGE 26.**

**Traditional**

Here we go! Your first song with 3 chords, the C, F, and G7. The best part of this song is that you only have to add one finger to go from the F to the G7 chord. There are many lyrics you can sing for this song, but we will just sing the first 2 verses.

**TUNING**

G C E G
4 3 2 1

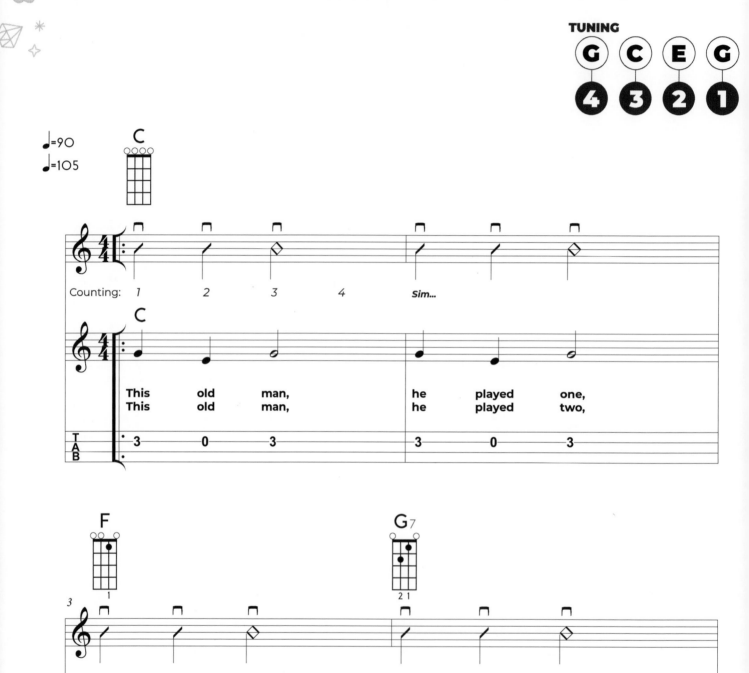

Counting: 1    2    3    4    *Sim...*

This    old    man,    he    played    one,
This    old    man,    he    played    two,

he    played    nick - nack    on    my    thumb,    with    a
he    played    nick - nack    on    my    shoe,    with    a

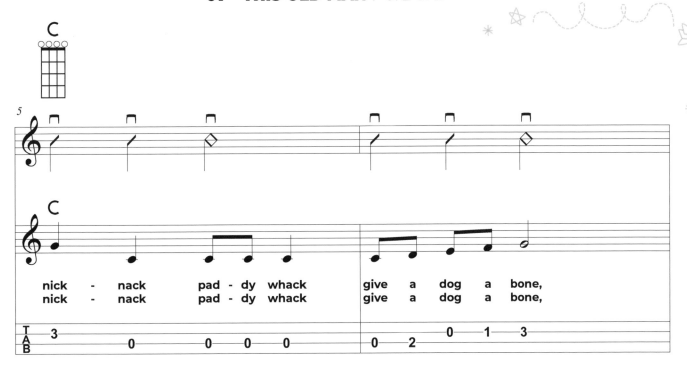

nick - nack pad - dy whack give a dog a bone,
nick - nack pad - dy whack give a dog a bone,

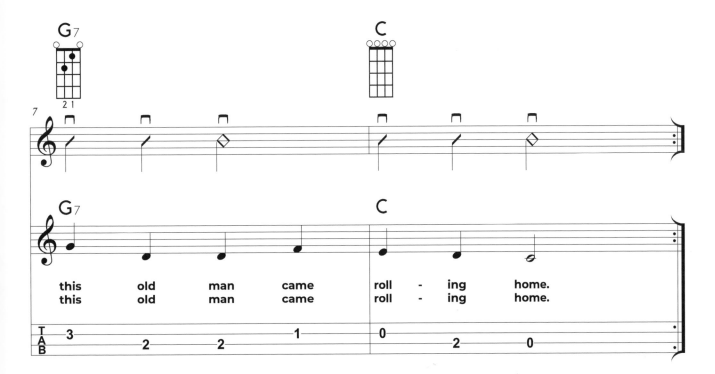

this old man came roll - ing home.
this old man came came roll - ing home.

You can post your progress and see how others are doing at the **UKELIKETHEPROS.COM** Forum.

You can also get free access to the backing tracks at:
**UKELIKETHEPROS.COM/KIDS-BOOK**

**Traditional**

This is one of my favorite songs to sing with my kids. This song uses the C and G7 chords, all downs-troke quarter notes, and a 1st and 2nd ending. Play the 1st ending and then after the repeat skip the 1st ending and play the 2nd ending. There is a vocal pickup on this song.

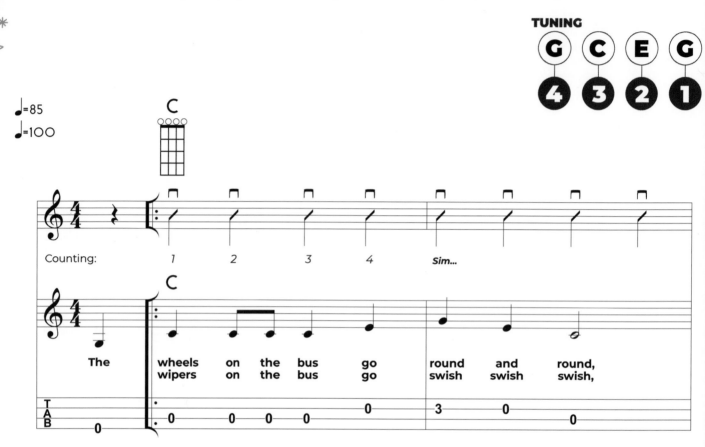

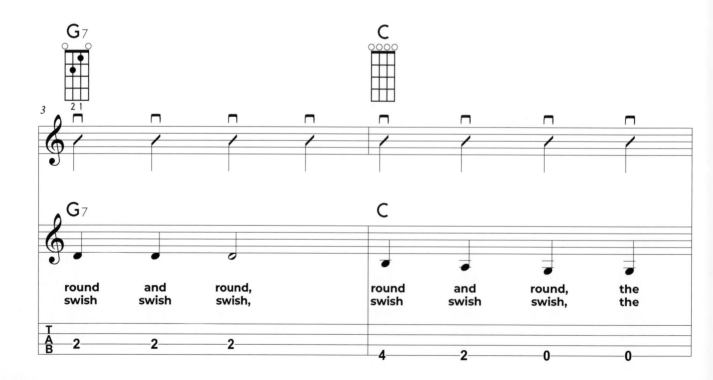

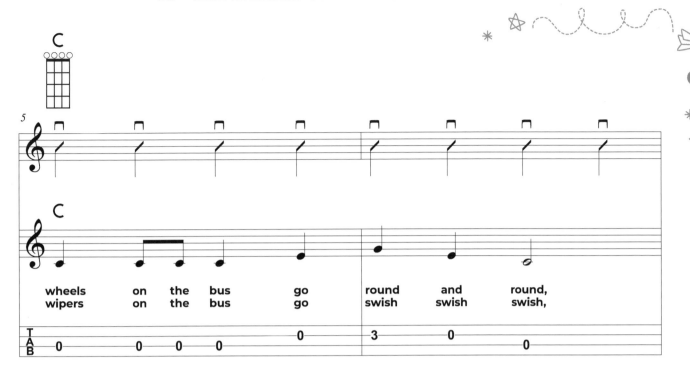

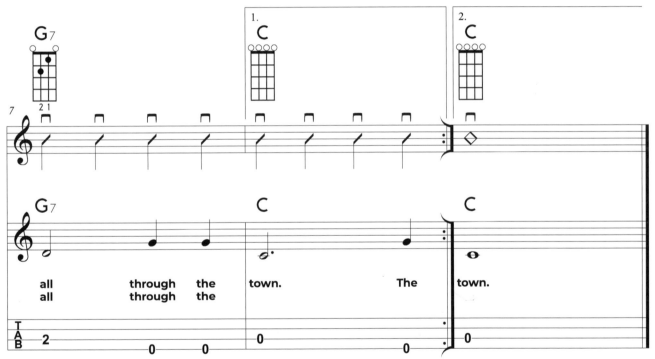

# PRO TIP

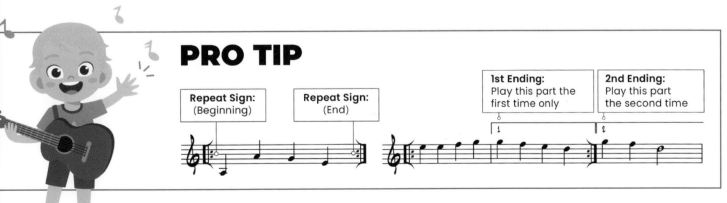

| Repeat Sign:<br>(Beginning) | Repeat Sign:<br>(End) | 1st Ending:<br>Play this part the<br>first time only | 2nd Ending:<br>Play this part<br>the second time |

## Traditional

E-I-E-I-O. And on his farm, he had a C, F, and G7 chord. In this fun song we will use all downstroke quarter strums while weaving between the C, F, and G7 chords. Memorize the chords for faster switching. We will sing the verses about the pig and the cow.

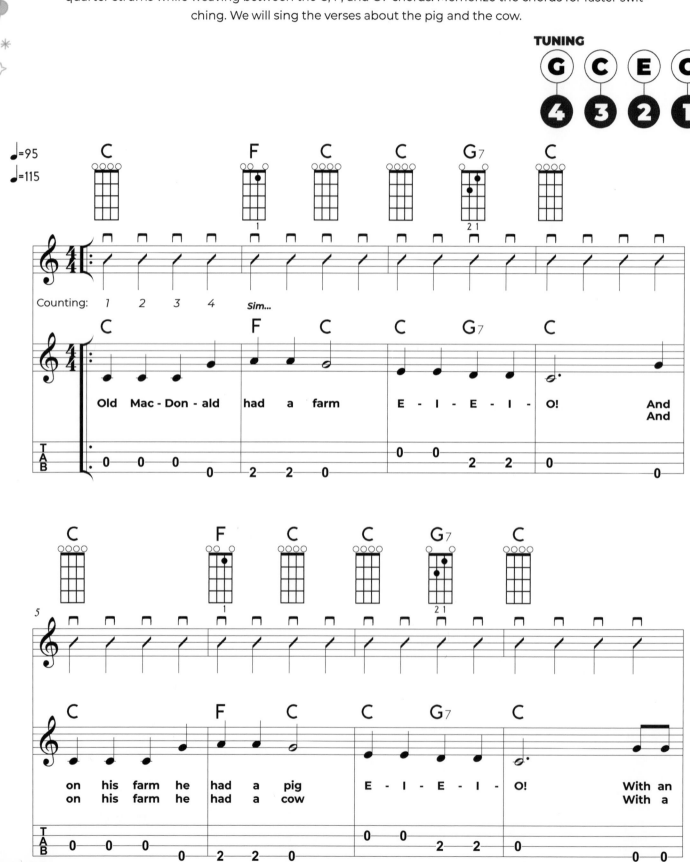

oink oink here, and an | oink oink there, | here an oink, there an oink, | Ev ery where an oink oink,
moo moo here, and a | moo moo there, | here a moo there a moo | Ev ery where a moo moo,

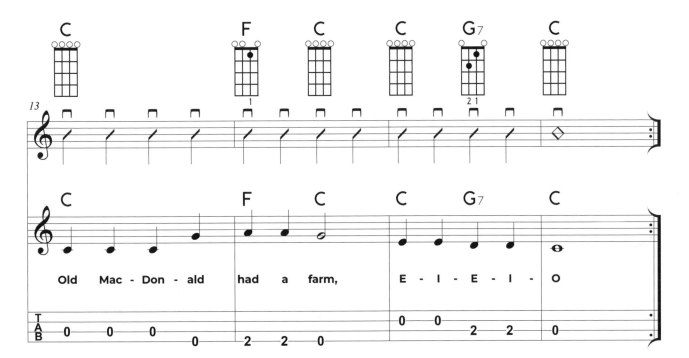

Old    Mac - Don - ald    had a    farm,    E - I - E - I - O

**Traditional**

This is the song where you will learn your first up stroke. You will use your index finger to strum the rhythm, down-down-up-down. On the up stroke lightly flick your finger up the strings with a light wrist. The up stroke will be indicated by the 'V' symbol.

**C**

Lon - don bridge is fall - ing down,

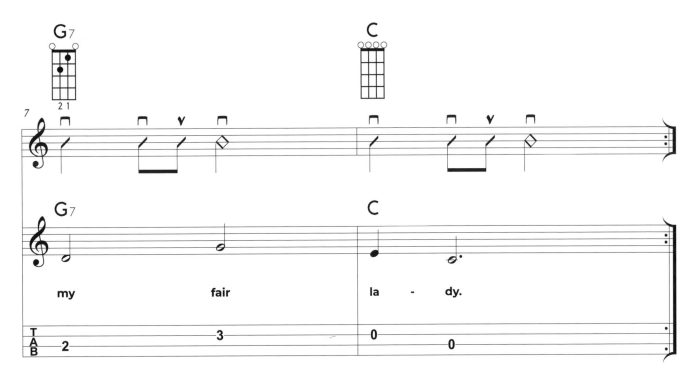

**G7** **C**

my fair la - dy.

You can post your progress and see how others are doing at the **UKELIKETHEPROS.COM** Forum.

You can also get free access to the backing tracks at: **UKELIKETHEPROS.COM/KIDS-BOOK**

**Traditional**

In this song we are going to use the same Down-Down-Up-Down strum pattern, but every other measure you have 2 chords in it. You will strum Down-Down-Up on the G7 chord, and then Down on the C chord on beat 3. There is also a vocal pickup on this one.

**TUNING**

G C E G
4 3 2 1

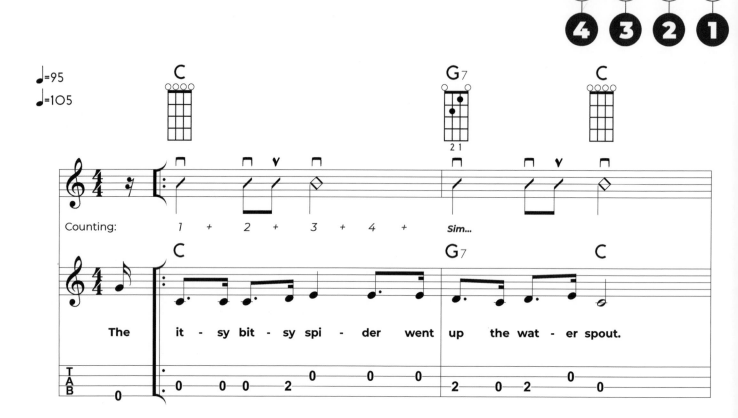

Counting: 1 + 2 + 3 + 4 + Sim...

The it - sy bit - sy spi - der went up the wat - er spout.

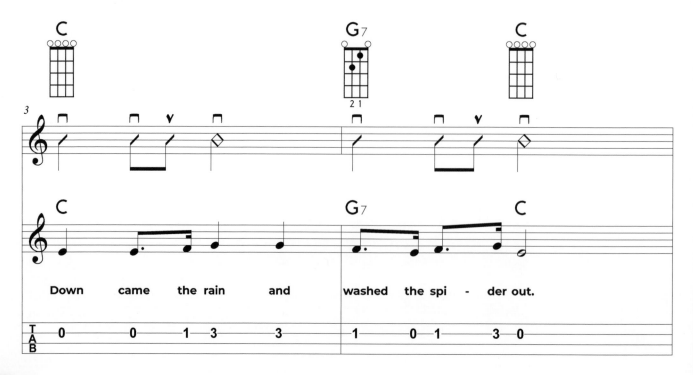

Down came the rain and washed the spi - der out.

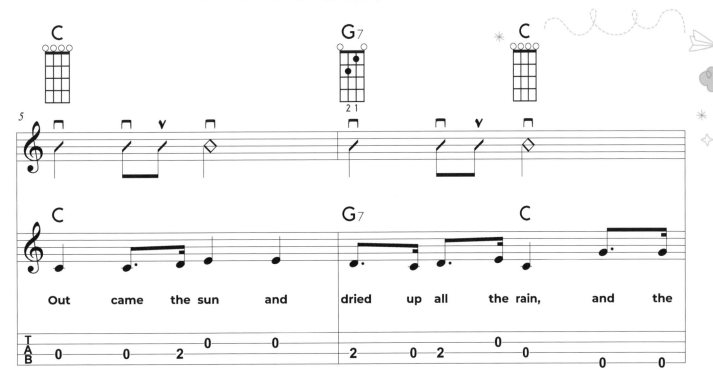

Out came the sun and dried up all the rain, and the

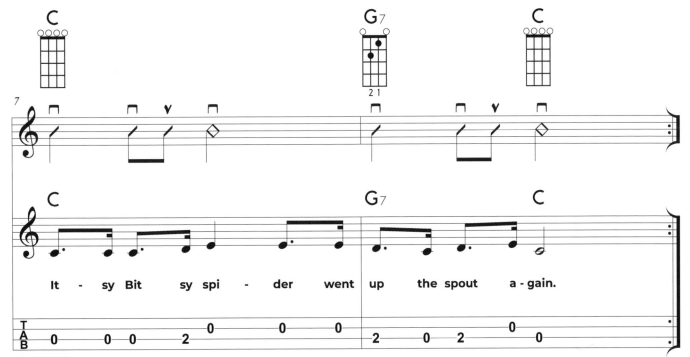

It - sy Bit - sy spi - der went up the spout a - gain.

You can post your progress and see how others are doing at the **UKELIKETHEPROS.COM** Forum.

You can also get free access to the backing tracks at: **UKELIKETHEPROS.COM/KIDS-BOOK**

**Traditional**

We've got 2 new things to learn in this song. First, you will learn the E minor chord, which is the same fingering as the G7 chord, but you slide your hand up to the 3rd fret. Second, you will learn a strum pattern that is Down-Down-Up-Down-Down.

thow 'em o'ver your shoul - der like a con - ti - nen - tal sol - dier? Do your

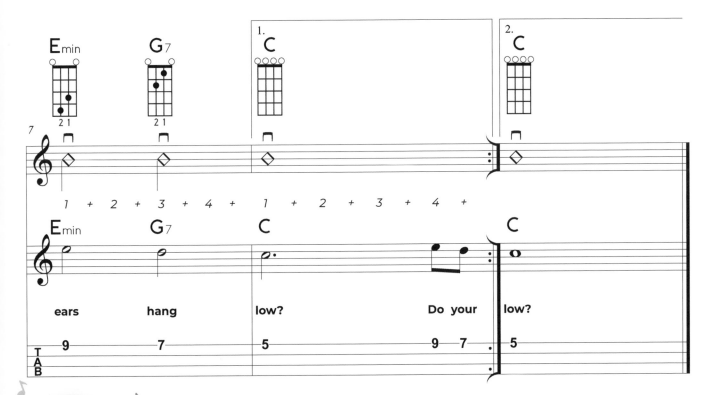

ears hang low? Do your low?

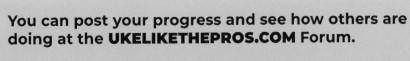

**Traditional**

In our final song we are going to use the C, F, and G7 chords, but we are going to use the 2-finger F chord. The 2-finger F chord starts like our regular F, but we will add our 2nd finger on the 2nd fret of the 4th string. You got this!

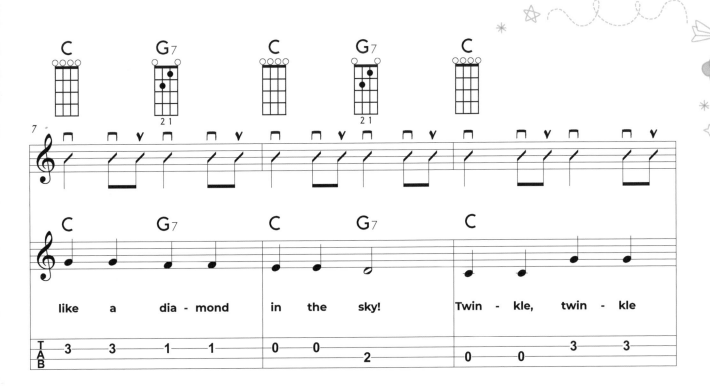

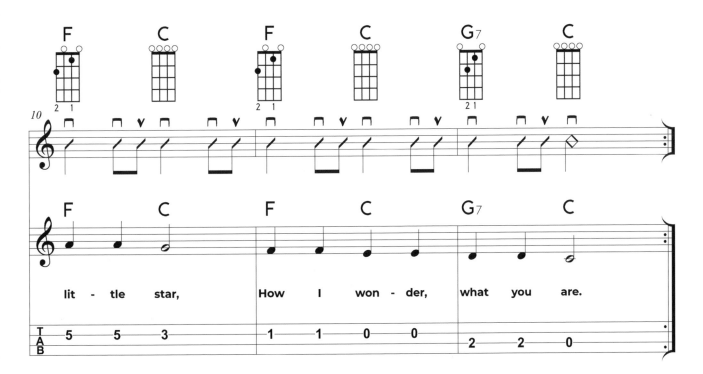

## Here are the answers from page 12:

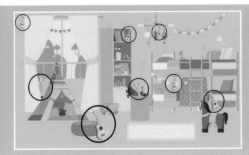 Were you able to find them all? Here are the exact places for each one of the ukuleles: 1. In the upper left corner of the curtain rod. 2. Behind the curtain. 3. Next to the cushion shaped like a car wheel. 4. In the highest space on the shelf. 5. Inside the place where toys are kept. 6. Hanging from the bedroom lamp. 7. Sleeping on the bottom bunk bed. 8. Behind the horse.

# GREAT Job!

YOU DID IT! Congratulations, you completed the Beginning Ukulele Kids Course Songbook. I'm so proud of you for making the commitment to learn the ukulele and play these fun songs. Continue to use this book as a resource, and work on always improving on these songs. You can always get better and you can always make it more challenging by playing at faster tempos or trying to sing while you play.

Did you have fun with these songs? Want to learn more ukulele?

Here at Uke Like The Pros, we love to teach you the ukulele, and nothing brings us more joy than seeing you improve your playing. At **ukelikethepros.com** we have a step-by-step path for you to follow so you know exactly which course will match your skill level. The next steps are the **Beginning Ukulele Starter Course**, the **Beginning Ukulele Bootcamp**, and then the famous **Master The Ukulele 1 Course**. If you are more of an Intermediate player, you can check out the **Beginning**

**Ukulele Fingerstyle Songbook**, the **Beginning Ukulele Blues Mastery Course**, or the **Beginning Ukulele Music Reading Course**.

If you want it all, you can join the Platinum Membership. The Platinum Membership gives you access to every course at ukelikethepros.com, including access to the member-only forum, weekly LIVE Q & A video calls, and VIP access to challenges and workshops. Check out the Platinum Membership at **ukelikethepros.com/platinum.**

I'm proud of you for completing the Beginning Ukulele Kids Course Songbook, and I look forward to connecting with you more at **ukelikethepros.com, terrycartermusicstore.com** and all the Uke Like The Pros social media channels.

Talk soon,
Terry Carter

# ABOUT THE AUTHOR

## TERRY CARTER

Terry Carter is a San Diego-based ukulele player, surfer, songwriter, and creator of ukelikethepros.com, rocklikethepros.com and terrycartermusicstore.com.

With over 25 years as a professional musician, educator and Los Angeles studio musician, Terry has worked with greats like Weezer, Josh Groban, Robby Krieger (The Doors), 2-time Grammy winning composer Christopher Tin (Calling All Dawns), Duff McKagan (Guns N' Roses), Grammy winning producer Charles Goodan (Santana/Rolling Stones), and the Los Angeles Philharmonic.

Terry has written and produced tracks for commercials (Discount Tire and Puma) and TV shows, including Scorpion (CBS), Pit Bulls & Parolees (Animal Planet), Trippin', Wildboyz, and The Real World (MTV). He has self-published over 10 books for Uke Like The Pros and Rock Like The Pros, filmed over 30 ukulele and guitar online courses and has over 140,000 subscribers on his Uke Like The Pros YouTube channel.

Terry received a Master of Music in Studio/Jazz Guitar Performance from University of Southern California and a Bachelor of Music from San Diego State University, with an emphasis in Jazz Studies and Music Education. He has taught at the University of Southern California, San Diego State University, Santa Monica College, Miracosta College, and Los Angeles Trade Tech College.

# ABOUT

## Guitars in the Classroom
### Better Learning through Music

## GUITARS IN THE CLASSROOM

GITC started as a beautiful idea to bring hands on music to general education teachers so they could become song leaders for learning. Thanks to business sponsors, supportive foundations, artists, amazing private individuals and a hard working board of directors, for 21 years, GITC faculty members have been training teachers in public schools from coast to coast to sing, play, write lyrics for learning and lead hands on music with public school elementary students. Over 15,000 teachers have trained with GITC and the goal is reaching about a million students each school year, serving students during their most formative years when foundational skills in speaking, reading, writing and thinking as well as interpersonal skills and emotional intelligence can grow quickly. **Uke Like The Pros** helps raise awareness and money for their free teacher training programs to get hands-on music into classrooms so students can learn any subject through the power of song. Their SmartStart Ukulele Method book first introduced learning ukulele in Open C for elementary teachers and students, and anyone working in education is welcome to enroll in their free programs at **guitarsintheclassroom.org**

Photos: Guitars in the Classroom

L

# ONLINE UKULELE COURSES

The perfect place to learn how to play Ukulele, Baritone Ukulele, Guitar and Guitarlele.

## ULTP Roadmap
## WHERE TO START?

**1) UKULELE BEGINNER**
A.   Beginning Ukulele Starter Course
B.   Beginning Ukulele Bootcamp Course
C.   Ukulele Fundamentals Course
D.   Ukulele Practice & Technique Course
E.   Master the Ukulele 1

**2) UKULELE INTERMEDIATE**
A.   Master The Ukulele 2
B.   Beginning Music Reading
C.   23 Ultimate Chord Progressions
D.   Beginning Ukulele Fingerstyle Course

**3) UKULELE ADVANCED**
A.   Ukulele Blues Mastery Course
B.   Beginning Ukulele Soloing Course
C.   Fingerstyle Mastery Course
D.   Jazz Swing Mastery Course

### MORE OPTIONS!

**FUNLAND**
A.   Beginning Ukulele Kids Course Songbook
B.   21 Popular Songs for Ukulele
C.   The Best Ukulele Christmas Songs
D.   10 Classic Rock Licks
E.   Guitar Fundamentals

**BARITONE UKULELE**
A.   Beginning Baritone Ukulele Bootcamp Course
B.   6 Weeks Baritone Q&A
C.   Baritone Blues Mastery Course
D.   Beginning Baritone Fingerstyle Course

**GUITARLELE**
A.   Guitarlele Starter Course
B.   6 Weeks Guitarlele Q&A
C.   Guitarlele Course for Ukulele and Guitar Players
D.   Guitarlele Blues Mastery Course

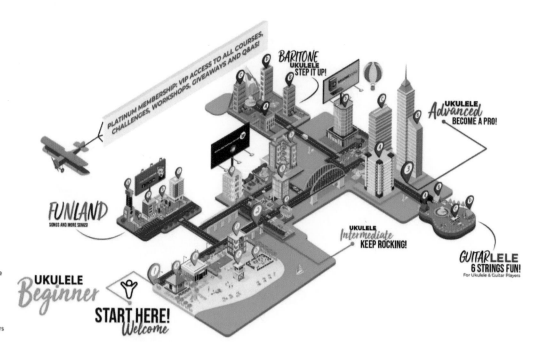

## Courses For All Levels
## UKELIKETHEPROS.COM

# TERRY CARTER MUSIC STORE

All your music needs at the #1 music store, **terrycartermusicstore.com**

Ukuleles

Guitars

Cases

Amplifiers and
Pedals

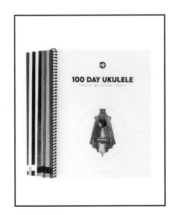

Books

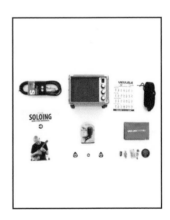

Accessories

UKELIKETHEPROS.COM
BLOG.UKELIKETHEPROS.COM
TERRYCARTERMUSICSTORE.COM

@ukelikethepros

INTERESTED IN **GUITAR CONTENT?**
**ROCKLIKETHEPROS.COM**

Printed in Great Britain
by Amazon

37758044R00027